THE CONSTELLATION URSA MAJOR

LISA OWINGS

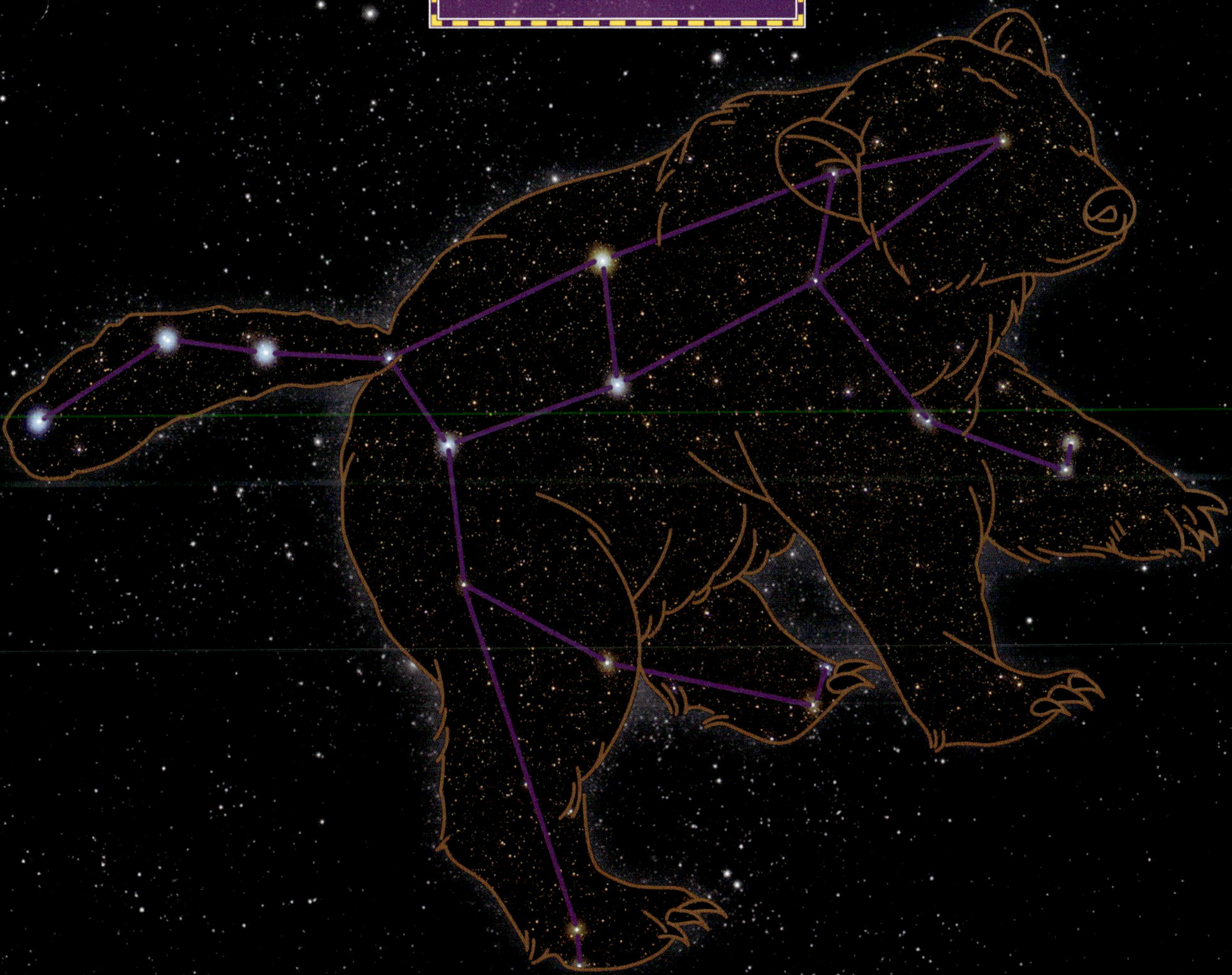

Published by The Child's World®
800-599-READ • www.childsworld.com

Photography Credits
Photographs ©: Shutterstock Images, cover (illustration), cover (background), 1 (illustration), 1 (background), 2 (illustration), 2–3, 9 (illustration), 11, 23, 24, 29; E. Slawik/NSF/AURA/M. Zamani/NOIRLab, cover (constellation), 1 (constellation), 2 (constellation), 9 (constellation); Evgeniy Bondar/Shutterstock Images, 5; IAU and Sky & Telescope/NOIRLab, 6; NASA, 10; Kelly vanDellen/Shutterstock Images, 13; Marianna Ianovska/Shutterstock Images, 14; Igor Golovniov/Shutterstock Images, 17; Fine Art Images/Heritage Images/Hulton Fine Art Collection/Getty Images, 18; Riccardo Sala/Alamy, 19; Maksim Belonenko/Shutterstock Images, 20; Holly Kuchera/Shutterstock Images, 27; Design elements from Shutterstock Images

ISBN Information
9781503875838 (Reinforced Library Binding)
9781503876255 (Portable Document Format)
9781503876873 (Online Multi-user eBook)
9781503877375 (Electronic Publication)

LCCN 2025938269

Printed in the United States of America

ABOUT THE AUTHOR

Lisa Owings has a degree in English and creative writing from the University of Minnesota. She has written and edited a wide variety of educational books for young people. Lisa lives in Andover, Minnesota, where Ursa Major is in the sky every night.

TABLE OF CONTENTS

CHAPTER ONE

The Constellation Ursa Major

Early humans had a special relationship with bears. Bears could be dangerous. Bears and humans sometimes competed for food, shelter, and other resources. But bears had surprising similarities to people. In addition to meat, bears ate berries and plants. They sometimes stood on two legs like people. Humans feared and hunted bears. But they also respected them.

These same ancient peoples watched the night sky. They tried to make sense of the shining stars. Slowly, people began to see shapes in the stars. These shapes are called constellations. One group of stars looked like a great bear. The star-bear circled the northern skies. Sometimes it seemed to stand on four legs and other times on two. This constellation became known as Ursa Major, the Great Bear. Ursa Minor, the Little Bear, is nearby.

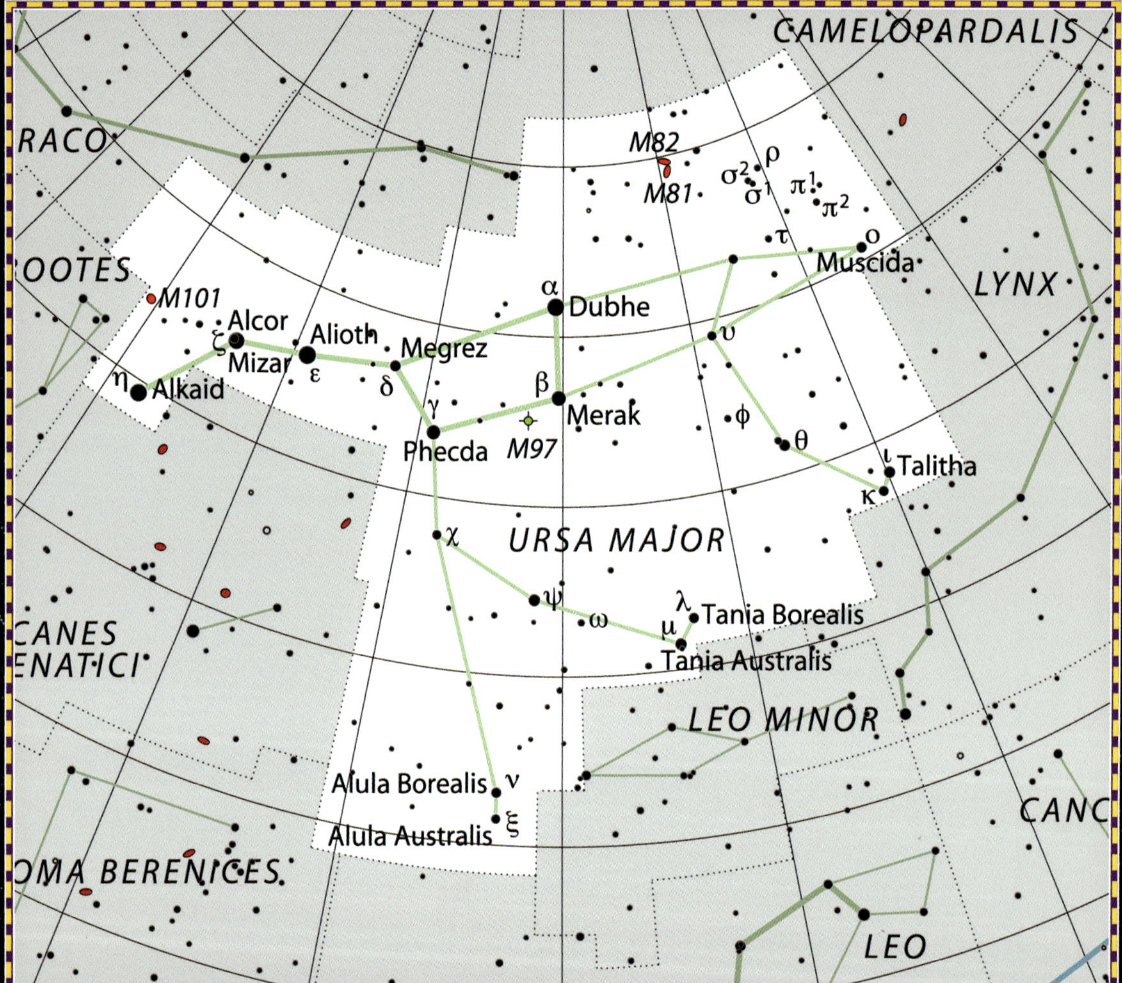

Every space object within the white area is considered part of Ursa Major.

Constellations are groups of stars that form pictures or patterns. They might look like animals, people, or tools. Constellations also include the sky around their shapes. This means every star in the sky is part of a constellation, even if it is not part of the constellation shape's outline. There are 88 official constellations recognized today. Ursa Major is the third largest of them.

The stars in the night sky look small. That is because they are so far away. Stars are actually giant balls of brightly burning gas. Some stars are bigger than others. The Sun is the closest star to Earth. To people on Earth, the Sun looks larger than other stars. But the largest known star is at least 2,000 times the size of the Sun! Some stars also burn brighter than others. Large, bright stars are the easiest to see at night.

The brightest stars of Ursa Major make up the Big Dipper. The Big Dipper is the best-known asterism. An asterism is a group of stars that is not an official constellation. There are seven main stars in the Big Dipper. The Big Dipper's curved handle is also Ursa Major's tail. At the end of the handle is the star Alkaid. Mizar and its companion star Alcor mark the middle of the handle. The last star in the handle is called Alioth. This is the Big Dipper's brightest star.

Four stars make up the dipper's bowl. These are Megrez, Dubhe, Merak, and Phecda. Dubhe is the brightest star in the bowl. It and Merak are called the Pointers. A line drawn from Merak through Dubhe points to Polaris. Polaris is the North Star. It sits above the North Pole. Polaris does not appear to move in the sky.

MIZAR AND ALCOR

Mizar and Alcor are sometimes called the horse and rider. People who look closely can see that they are two separate stars. It is easier to see with binoculars or a telescope. But there is more to this pair than meets the eye. Mizar was the first known double star. What appears as one star is actually two stars that orbit each other. And each of Mizar's stars is a double star as well. This means Mizar is made of four stars. Alcor is also a double star. There are six total stars in the horse and rider.

There are 19 main stars in Ursa Major, not counting Alcor.

The other stars in Ursa Major are harder to see. A triangle of stars near the dipper's bowl marks the front part of the bear. Other stars create Ursa Major's legs and paws.

Johann Elert Bode discovered M82 in 1774.

Not all objects that shine in the night sky are stars. Some are planets. Others are **galaxies**. Many galaxies can be found in Ursa Major. M81 is one of the brightest galaxies in the sky. It sits above the bear's shoulders. It is also known as Bode's Galaxy. M82 hovers nearby. This galaxy looks a bit like a bird with spread wings. Above the bear's tail is M101, the Pinwheel Galaxy.

Ursa Major is also home to **nebulae**. The Owl Nebula glows faintly within Ursa Major. Its circular cloud has two dark patches. Some people think they look like large eyes in an owl's face.

The Owl Nebula's dark spots are only visible through a telescope.

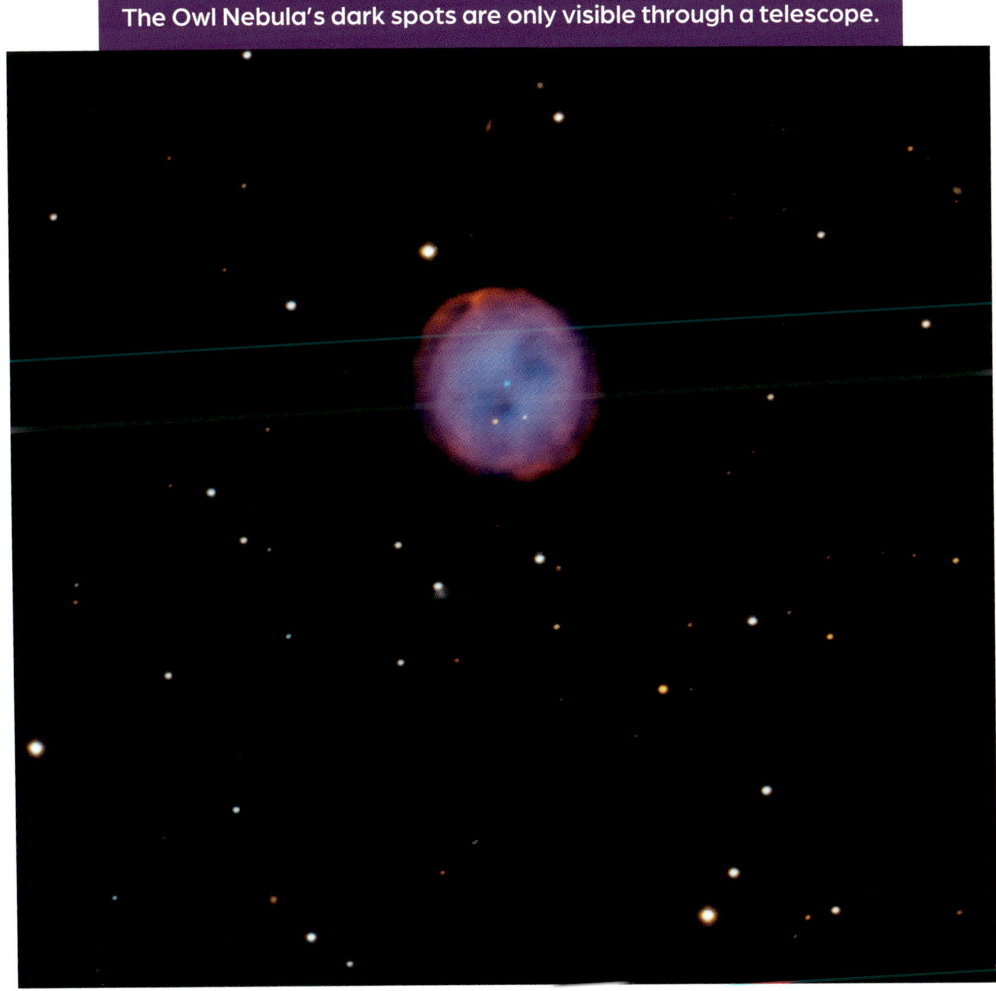

CHAPTER TWO

The Origin of the Myth

Ursa Major is said to be the oldest constellation. No one knows exactly when people grouped these stars together. It may have happened more than 14,000 years ago. The original constellation included only the stars of the Big Dipper. Many people knew it as a wagon or a **plow**. But other ancient people saw a bear. Stories of the constellation as a bear exist across Europe, Asia, and North America. For most, the bowl of the Big Dipper was the bear. The three stars of its handle were fierce hunters. They chased the bear forever through the skies. Others saw the whole dipper as a bear. But this bear had a very long tail. Real bears have short tails.

There are eight kinds of bears.
They all have short tails.

ARCADIA

Gods and goddesses were part of everyday life in ancient Greece. Zeus was the most powerful god. Many Greeks claimed to be related to him. Callisto's story is especially important to the Greeks who lived in the region of Arcadia. Zeus and Callisto's son, Arcas, is said to be the father of the Arcadians. Through Arcas, they can trace their history back to Zeus.

Stories of the star-bear have been told since long before people could write them down. But the Greeks shaped the story told today. The Greeks told a story of a hunter named Callisto. The mighty god Zeus fell in love with her. Eventually, Callisto was transformed into a bear. Some stories said Zeus's wife, Hera, was jealous of Callisto. She changed the hunter into a bear. Other stories say Artemis, the goddess of the hunt, transformed her. And some stories say Zeus did it. There are many versions. But in all of them, Zeus flung the she-bear into the sky. He threw her by her tail, which is why Ursa Major's tail is so long.

Greek **astronomers** knew the bear constellation well. The Greek poet Homer wrote of the bear almost 3,000 years ago. He noted that its stars never sank below the **horizon**. Ptolemy (TAH-luh-mee) was a Greco-Roman astronomer. In AD 150, he wrote a book about constellations. Ptolemy recognized 48 constellations. Most of these are included in the 88 constellations recognized today. Ursa Major was one of Ptolemy's original constellations.

CHAPTER THREE

The Story of Ursa Major

One day, Callisto went hunting in the forest. The beautiful **maiden** hunted all morning. By noon, the day had become hot. Callisto was tired. She went deep into the forest to find a shady place to rest. Callisto carefully set down her bow and **quiver** full of arrows. Then she lay in the soft grass. She used her quiver as a pillow.

Zeus, king of the gods, caught sight of her. The goddess Hera was his wife and queen. But Zeus fell in love with Callisto's beauty. He did not want to frighten the young hunter. So he took the form of Artemis, the goddess of the hunt. Callisto was one of Artemis's close companions.

Zeus tricked Callisto into thinking he was her friend Artemis.

Callisto woke to find her friend nearby. The two began to talk. After a while, Zeus could hide no longer. He revealed himself and his true feelings. Callisto was confused. She had promised Artemis that she would never love a man. But Zeus was very powerful, and Callisto could not refuse him. She became his companion. Then Zeus left. Callisto was alone.

Callisto tried to go back to her normal life. But soon her secret was revealed. One day, Artemis and her companions were taking a bath. Callisto did not want to join them. But Artemis told her to. When Callisto undressed, her companions realized she was pregnant. Artemis was furious. Callisto had broken her promise! Artemis banished the hunter. Callisto went away. She eventually gave birth to her son, Arcas.

In some stories, Artemis turns Callisto into a bear as soon as she discovers Callisto's pregnancy.

Some storytellers say Zeus was the one to turn Callisto into a bear. He was trying to hide her from Hera. But in many stories, Hera turned Callisto into a bear out of jealousy.

Before long, Hera found out what her husband had done. The queen of gods was wild with jealousy. She quickly found Callisto. Hera grabbed her by the hair. She dragged the lovely hunter to the ground. Callisto begged the goddess to forgive her. But even as Callisto spoke, dark fur spread down her arms and legs. Her fingernails curled into sharp claws. Her pleading words turned into fearsome growls. Callisto was horrified. She had become a bear!

Stories give different explanations of what happened to Arcas. In some stories, the god Hermes (pictured) rescues Arcas and brings him to Maia, Hermes's mother. In others, hunters bring Arcas to King Lycaon, Callisto's father.

Callisto roamed the forest in fear. The hunter had become the hunted. She fled from her friends' arrows on four legs. Sometimes she forgot she was a bear. When other bears or beasts passed by, she hid. Callisto also missed her son.

THE OTHER MYTH OF URSA MAJOR

Some Greeks told a different story about Ursa Major. They said she was Adrasteia. This goddess helped care for the young Zeus. Zeus's father wanted to kill him. So Zeus's mother hid him in an island cave. Adrasteia and her sister Ida cared for and protected baby Zeus. When Zeus grew up, he set them in the sky as the Great and Little Bears.

Years passed. Arcas grew into a young man. He became a skilled hunter, as his mother had been. But he did not remember her. One day, Arcas took his bow and arrow into the forest. Suddenly he saw a patch of fur through the trees. He crept closer. Then he drew back in fright. It was a bear! And it had seen him!

In fact, the bear was staring at him. Arcas did not understand why the beast was behaving so strangely. Why did it not run away? Instead, the bear moved toward him. Its huffs and growls were terrible and threatening. The bear was going to attack! Arcas raised his weapon. He pointed it at the bear's chest, ready to strike a deadly blow. He had no way of knowing that this bear was his beloved mother, desperate to show him love.

Just then, Zeus appeared. He stopped Arcas from shooting. Then he turned the boy into a bear. Now Arcas could recognize his mother. In this form, the two could be together. They would never be apart again.

Arcas did not recognize his mother.

Callisto and Arcas were reunited in the sky.

Zeus grabbed each bear by the tail. Then he swung them high into the heavens. Their tails stretched out where Zeus had pulled them. Their stars lit up the whole night sky. There they would stay forever, the Great Bear and the Little Bear.

Hera's anger once again burned hot. How could her husband give Callisto such an honored place? How dare he make her queen of the night sky! Hera complained to the sea gods. She begged them not to let Callisto or her son bathe in their waters. The sea gods obeyed Hera's request. This is why the Great and Little Bears never dip below the horizon into the ocean's waves.

CHAPTER FOUR

The Myth of Ursa Major in Other Cultures

Some Native American peoples saw a bear in Ursa Major's stars. But they told different stories than the Greeks. A Mohawk story tells of three brothers hunting a bear. They chased the bear into the sky. The stars in the Big Dipper's handle are the brothers. A Zuni story also recognizes the bear. Its rising means spring is coming. Some Native American stories explain Alcor, Mizar's companion star. A Mi'kmaq story describes the Big Dipper's handle as three hunters. The middle hunter is carrying a pot in which to cook the bear. This pot is Alcor. In a Blackfoot story, a woman changes into a bear. She chases seven brothers and their sister. The **siblings** escape into the sky. The brothers became the stars of the Big Dipper. The sister became Alcor.

In the Ojibwe story, a fisher saves the world from evil ogres.

Not all stories saw Ursa Major as a bear. Ojibwe stargazers see a fisher in the stars of Ursa Major. A fisher is an animal related to the weasel. Ancient Egyptians saw Ursa Major's brightest stars as an animal's thigh. In India, the stars of the Big Dipper represent the Seven Sages. The sages, or wise men, have an important role in Hindu stories. Many cultures saw Ursa Major as a wagon or plow. Chinese astronomers saw the emperor's **chariot**. Arab astronomers saw another asterism in Ursa Major. Its feet created the Three Leaps of the Gazelle. The gazelle left its tracks in the sky as it ran from a nearby lion constellation.

CHAPTER FIVE

How to Find Ursa Major in the Sky

Ursa Major is always present in the Northern **Hemisphere**. It can be hard to make out its whole shape. But the Big Dipper is easy to find. Face north. Then look for its seven bright stars. If the night is clear, search next to the dipper's bowl for the bear's nose. Then look for the pairs of stars that mark its paws.

The Great Bear is highest in the sky in the spring. But it is also upside down. In fall, the bear is right-side up but low on the horizon. Some say it is looking for a place to spend the winter. But the Great Bear always spends winters in the sky. In winter and summer, it seems to stand on its hind legs. It is the closest the bear ever gets to human form.

GLOSSARY

astronomers (uh-STRAW-nuh-murz) Astronomers are scientists who study stars and other objects in space. Astronomers have recognized Ursa Major for thousands of years.

chariot (CHAYR-ee-uht) A chariot is a small vehicle pulled by horses. Chinese astronomers saw a chariot in Ursa Major.

galaxies (GAL-uhk-seez) Galaxies are groups of dust, gases, and billions of stars held together by gravity. Bode's Galaxy and the Pinwheel Galaxy are some of the galaxies found in Ursa Major.

hemisphere (HEH-mih-sfeer) A hemisphere is half of a sphere. Earth is divided into the Northern Hemisphere and Southern Hemisphere.

horizon (huh-RYE-zin) The horizon is the line where the ground or water seems to meet the sky. Ursa Major never sets below the horizon in the Northern Hemisphere.

maiden (MAY-den) A maiden is an unmarried woman or girl. Callisto was a beautiful maiden who was a hunter.

nebulae (NEH-byoo-lee) Nebulae are clouds of gas and dust in space where stars are born. The Owl's Head Nebula is one of the nebulae in Ursa Major.

orbit (OR-bit) To orbit an object is to move in a rounded path around it. The stars in a double star orbit each other.

plow (PLOW) A plow is a tool used to break up soil before seeds are planted. Some cultures saw a plow in Ursa Major.

quiver (KWIH-vur) A quiver is a container for holding arrows. Callisto carried a quiver when she went hunting.

siblings (SIH-blingz) Siblings are people who share a parent or parents, such as brothers and sisters. In a Blackfoot story, the Big Dipper was created by eight siblings who were chased into the sky by a bear.

FAST FACTS

- Constellations are groupings of stars in the sky that form pictures. Stars are glowing balls of gas throughout the universe. The Sun is a star.
- Ursa Major is the third-largest constellation. It is always above the horizon in the Northern Hemisphere.
- An asterism is a shape within a constellation. The Big Dipper is an asterism in Ursa Major.
- Ursa Major may be the oldest constellation. Cultures from around the world recognized the constellation as a bear.
- In Greek mythology, Callisto was a hunter. She was transformed into a bear by Zeus, Artemis, or Hera, depending on the story. Zeus hurled the bear into the sky by its tail. This is why the bear's tail is so long.
- Some Native American stories described hunters chasing a bear instead of a bear with a long tail. Stories from other cultures describe a wagon, a plow, a chariot, or wise men.

ONE STRIDE FURTHER

- Cultures around the world have different stories about Ursa Major. Which story do you find the most interesting? Why?
- In the Greek story, Ursa Major and Ursa Minor are Callisto and her son. Do you think becoming constellations was a happy ending for them? Why or why not?
- The next time you are outside on a clear night, look up to the stars. Imagine new constellations of your own. Would you create a different shape out of Ursa Major's stars?

FIND OUT MORE

IN THE LIBRARY

Owings, Lisa. *The Constellation Ursa Minor.* Parker, CO: The Child's World, 2026.

Patel, Parshati. *My Book of Stars and Planets.* New York, NY: DK Publishing, 2021.

Tracosas, L. J. *Ultimate Greek Mythology.* New York, NY: Z Kids, 2023.

ON THE WEB

Visit our website for links about Ursa Major:

childsworld.com/links

Note to Parents, Caregivers, Teachers, and Librarians: We routinely verify our web links to make sure they are safe and active sites. So encourage your readers to check them out!

INDEX